MW00803365

Viewfindings

Slivers of light in a tempestuous time

Melody Mociulski

Edited by Jacoba Lawson.
Designed by Wayne Kehoe.
Contact info@waynekehoe.com

Thank you, dear sister Lizanne, for believing in me and encouraging me to make this book – and, most of all, for your love.

Preface

March 2021. Our world is acknowledging the one-year anniversary of the COVID-19 pandemic. Today, the world reports 121,516,034 confirmed cases and 2,685,908 deaths, of which 536,472 occurred in the United States.

When Covid "officially" started in 2020, most of the world went into lockdown. We were told by our governments that the pandemic would be harnessed within a month or so. Some countries took lockdown requirements more seriously than others. We were all told that we could do our part to stop the virus spread by staying home, wearing masks in public, and washing our hands constantly. No vaccine was available, and the molecular makeup of this virus was not yet identified.

History will remember this as a time when the planet's entire populace took a timeout from life. With fewer negative human-inflicted environmental impacts, the animal kingdom and nature, not affected by Covid, thrived.

Everyone was home isolating. Businesses closed, except for essentials like grocery stores and pharmacies. Store shelves were frequently empty as folks purchased extra toilet paper and foods "just in case." Schools closed, and parents learned to teach their children at home while they themselves worked from home. Each person's individual risk assessment determined their lockdown behavior. No one thought this new normal could last for long.

When Washington State mandated its lockdown, the beauty of spring beckoned. I decided to purposefully take photos on Bainbridge Island during walks and bike rides. It provided me with a mission and a reason to be outside in nature. I challenged myself to post two photos to Facebook every day for fifty days—no text, no context, just photos. I captured whatever caught my eye while out and about, creating an eclectic assortment of photos. This project gave me a creative purpose during the early days of the pandemic.

Summer came and new Covid cases and deaths continued. Politics in red states and blue states determined economic reopening ventures, some resulting in super-spreader outbreaks and renewed lockdowns. Life slowed down for everyone except essential workers forced to take risks to serve the greater need. Hospitals become overloaded and medical personnel burned out. Though funerals were not allowed, the names of the fallen were remembered.

On the home front, yards flourished with blooming color. Home projects, usually neglected, received the attention and energy of whole families. Jigsaw puzzles, bread baking, and TV streaming became the rage. The days were still long and the weather warm. We adapted to a slower pace of life, appreciated quality time with our children, and became more tolerant of each other.

And then it was fall. Covid cases and deaths continued to increase daily around the world . Our homes, previously seen as a safe harbor for refuge without masks, began to feel like claustrophobic cages. We felt emotionally exhausted by this pandemic. We wanted to hug each other, see grandchildren, attend weddings, eat in restaurants, and plan vacations. All these acts we'd previously taken for granted were still beyond reach.

When the first vaccines were approved and administered to patients in December 2020, there was a collective sigh of relief around the globe. It felt like there was finally some light at the end of this torturous tunnel. Yes, the world still needed more time to produce and distribute the vaccines, and convince at least 90 percent of the populace to accept them for successful global herd immunity. However, it finally felt like there was hope.

Collectively, the world's 7 billion people experienced this pandemic together, but each of us has our own unique story. What did each of us see, feel, suffer, and learn? How did each of us survive? How will our life and priorities shift moving forward? This book represents my story and my perspective. I am grateful that my story is not one of Covid death. However, like many others, it was a year of caretaking for family members facing severe physical and mental challenges and personal anxiety caused by volatile politics and injustices. My mental survival became dependent on my ability to focus on the joy and hope still present in our world. I turned to meditation for the first time in my life. This pathway to peace of mind and gratitude saved me.

In the midst of winter's dark days, still isolating, still fearing infection, my dear sister suggested that I challenge myself once again. This time, the challenge was to share the photos I took at the beginning of Covid and describe what those captured moments mean to me now, as I reflect on how the pandemic changed my priorities.

Having just turned seventy-four, I am more aware of mortality than ever. Making this book and immersing myself in the process has been my survival lifeline during Covid. As the world begins to reopen, I hope I will remember to witness and appreciate the precious beauty of life each day. I hope I will continue to fill myself with gratitude for this opportunity at life, my good health, and my beloved family and friends. I believe this book will help me to remember.

To help you visualize the context for these photos, allow me to set the scene. Bainbridge—an island about the size of Manhattan—is a thirty-five-minute ferry ride from Seattle, Washington. It is a small-town, rural community of about 26,000 people. We are blessed with considerable access to walking trails, boating opportunities, and bicycle paths. The island is a favorite getaway for mainland locals and tourists visiting Seattle.

This book represents one voice, one year, one island, and one eye's view. The year 2020 was full of unprecedented pain, loss, death, fear, and anger. The pandemic has taken a toll on everyone in the world. I hope this collection of memories will act as a reminder that even in the midst of crisis, there is a bounty of beauty and wonder all around us that can bring joy to our hearts and hope to our souls.

Clouds

Dreams sitting on a cloud

Soft billowing pillows

Ever changing

Always moving, drifting, gliding

Revealing the silver lining

Ambling rainbows

Hyacinths at dawn

Twilight pink petals

Menacing shadows molding nature's fury

Wonders cast from the heavens

Dancing on air

Witnessing the magic

Magnificent universe

Dedicated to my birth mom Betty

Stillness

This bicyclist is utterly frozen in motion. Free from chaos, she is taking a break to soak up the still waters of Eagle Harbor.
She is calm in the moment, savoring the sounds of the gulls and breathing the freshness of the sea air. Like me, she is at a phase of her life where she actively seeks serenity.

"Even in stillness, there is movement. Sometimes it takes time for the molecules of change to shift form. Even when it feels like nothing is happening, transformation is taking place."

—Anonymous

Ride

Bike riding on hilly Bainbridge Island is a workout and a joy. With both Mt. Rainier and Seattle in the distance, this downhill stretch is always stunning.

Bainbridge is home to the Chilly Hilly event, which kicks off the Pacific Northwest cycling season each year. This thirty-three mile race, held on the last Sunday in February for over forty years, draws upwards of 6,000 riders. Aptly named, its weather is always unpredictable and its 2,675 feet of hill climbing are a challenge. I haven't yet had the courage to take it on.

"Nothing compares to the simple pleasure of riding a bike."

—John F. Kennedy

Dance

Nature truly comes to life in the spring. New growth peeks out of the ground. Birds chatter. Days grow longer. Temperatures rise. It's a sign that the world will soon be covered in color again. Every spring is a new beginning.

I believe that nature speaks to us. Spring blossoms dance in a light breeze, performing a rousing rhumba, a slow waltz, or a jazzy jitterbug. This spectacular poppy says it is time for a sexy salsa.

"Spring is nature's way of saying, 'Let's party!"

—Robin Williams

Spirits

Remnants of a family's craft project positioned randomly along the sidewalk? Or strategically placed amulets warding off evil and suffering?

The crocodile spirit wears a crown of strength, arm rings of honor, and a powerful magic belt for protection. The attending amulets add vigilance.

Totems like these tell us we cannot always be docile and gentle. Rather, we must also possess courage, patience, and honor, especially in times of crisis. Especially in times like these.

"See you later, alligator. After a while, crocodile."

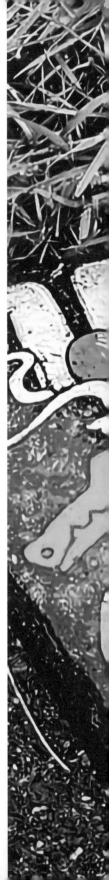

Listen

Walking along this trail in the early morning's fresh rain, I hear the chirpy chatter of birds and the running waters of the swollen creek. My mind calms. I am reminded of the power of listening.

According to ecologist Bernie Krause, every habitat has its own 'unique auditory signature'. This imprint includes sounds made by living things, non-biological sounds like wind, water, and waves, and sounds created by humans. All we have to do is stop and listen for them.

Whether I am listening to nature or listening to my husband, I try to devote my full attention, recognizing that it is not necessarily easy. Yet, being listened to is a powerful gift.

"Trees are sanctuaries. Whoever knows how to speak to them, whoever knows how to listen to them, can learn the truth. They do not preach learning and precepts, they preach, undeterred by particulars, the ancient law of life."

—Hermann Hesse, Wandering

Quaint

Port Madison boathouse

Appealingly quaint

Reminiscent of boating-day lore.

Seafaring yarns

Secrets untold

If the timbers could talk

Memories galore.

Port Madison boathouse

Still standing strong

Shelter from storms

Dripping with charm

Stowing tales from before.

Community

Town & Country grocery first opened on Bainbridge Island in 1957. In 2014, they started a major yearlong renovation. They never closed. We customers felt like part of the process as we wandered the aisles in search of items that were constantly being moved. T&C has been the heart of our community for sixty-three years. A quick run to the store is impossible, as we inevitably run into friends. We always know we can find whatever we want at T&C, and the staff are like family.

When Covid lockdown started in March 2020, T&C took an active role. And the community immediately stepped up to make masks for all employees to keep them safe while they supported us customers.

Bainbridge residents tend to respect each other's rights and health. With Covid, we seriously follow our state's guidelines— wearing masks, maintaining social distance, and adhering to lockdown directives. Only 216 residents out of over 26,000 have tested positive since January 2020.

"The greatness of a community is most accurately measured by the compassionate actions of its members."

—Coretta Scott King

Defense

Fort Ward, at the southern tip of Bainbridge Island, played a significant role in both World Wars. It happened that this spot was an outstanding location for eavesdropping on radio communications transmitted from Japan, and it developed into a top-secret military listening post.

The US Army abandoned all operations in 1958. Today, extensive walking trails, stunning water access, and deserted artillery batteries make it a favorite destination for visitors and locals.

"Heroism doesn't always happen in a burst of glory. Sometimes small triumphs and large hearts change the course of history."

—Mary Roach, *Grunt: The Curious Science of Humans at War*

Port Blakely

Port Blakely, also known as Blakely Harbor on southeast Bainbridge Island, came to life in 1863. An active sawmilling town, it boasted the highest-producing sawmill in the world for a while. Prone to fires, it burned to the ground in 1888 and again in 1907. Rebuilt each time, it finally closed in 1924.

In a little town so still

There's a building old and battered

Tis the old saw-mill.

It is twisted, it is tattered

From the toil of many years

The walls are scratched and shattered

Yet it shows no sign of fear.

The carriage growls and grumbles

As it journeys to and fro,

And the engine howls and mumbles

Making all the pullies go.

—excerpt from "The Old Saw Mill," author unknown

Connect

The year 2020 was tough for everyone. Covid, loss of personal contact, politics, natural disasters, and the economic downturn.

I finally turned to meditation after years of intending but failing to try it. Acquiring a tool to quiet the constant chatter in my head has been life changing. I never really understood what it meant to "be present" or "connect" with myself. Taped to my computer is a reminder: "Let go of the past. Connect with yourself. Wake up. Be present."

It is definitely easier said than done.

Connecting with others has not been easy within Covid constraints. Yet we humans need each other. I hope we will be able to connect and hug again in 2021.

"The most basic and powerful way to connect to another person is to listen. Just listen. A loving silence often has far more power to heal and to connect than the most well-intentioned words."

—Rachel Naomi Remen

Tides

A lone wolf crying to the moon

slivers of light skipping on the tides

in and out again and again.

neap tides, spring tides

high tides, low tides

soothingly predictable

silvery full moon

pulling at our earth

ruling the tides

higher and higher

building intensity

crashing tides

ebb and flow

coming in, peaking, passing

waves of emotion

passing through me

my inner ocean

Serenity

Walking in the early morning light is magical. Everything looks better and feels better. And in spring, the lush new growth begins revealing its face once again. It's a new day, a new beginning.

"You can't calm the storm, so stop trying. What you can do is calm yourself. The storm will pass."

—*Timber Hawkeye*

Peace

Meditation uses many ocean visuals. Conjure peacefulness while gazing at the vast waters. Allow the cycles of waves flowing in and out to remind you that this too shall pass.

I think of myself as a small speck in the huge universe of life, a tiny drop of water in the ocean's expanse. Yet, we carry in our hearts and souls all our experiences, all those we have lost, and all our dreams. Rumi believed we each carry our world inside of us. In his words, "You are not a drop in the ocean. You are the entire ocean in a drop."

Cycles

Cycles of life surround us. Planetary movements cycle. Seasons cycle, as do weather, nature, and the ocean tides. Our bodies reflect endless cycles for breathing, blood flow, and functioning of minute cells in our systems.

On a more mundane level, ferries connecting Bainbridge Island to Seattle leave every 50–60 minutes. These cycles determine how abruptly we leave a party to "catch the boat."

"I think the reason the world is a mystical, enchanting place, is because of the cycle of life. My body will decompose, but maybe some little element of it will be transformed into a particle of dirt, over years and years, and then a glorious flower will be nurtured by this particle of dirt. Then this flower will nourish a random bumblebee, who in turn will be eaten by a raven. So, in some future life, I'll be able to fly. I look forward to that. I've always admired the freedom of birds."

— E. M. Crane

Quiet

Remembering the quiet streets of early Covid-2020 lockdown brings me a smile and fond memories. Bike rides were so much safer without traffic. I could hear the happy chatter of birds everywhere. Waters surrounding our island were cleaner. Air smelled fresh all the time. Strangers smiled more. Sleep patterns improved. In hindsight, even with the Covid adjustments and fears, it was an exquisite time in this journey.

Why does quiet feel comforting? Experts believe that precious moments of quiet still our minds. In today's fast paced world, my mind rarely slows down. When I consciously find quiet time, especially during meditation, I feel rejuvenated and more in touch with what truly matters in my life.

"Learn to be quiet enough to hear the genuine within yourself so that you can hear it in others."

— Marian Wright Edelman

Haven

Hear the raven

Singing toc-toc-toc.

Black as oil

Bronze sparks

Glistening in the sun.

Seeking a haven

Flights steeped with grace

Soaring low over water

Finding the perfect place.

Singing toc-toc-toc.

Passion

According to Kevin Hall, passion is more than a barely controllable emotion. This renowned word expert describes it as "a willingness to suffer for what you love." Compassion, therefore, is "a willingness to suffer with another."

My passion is empowering women and girls with education. I truly believe women and girls can improve our world if they are given the opportunity and tools. When I founded Educational Empowerment in 2012, I finally understood compassion's powerful driving force. Although fraught with obstacles, this journey has brought me unimaginable joy and fulfillment. I only wish I had recognized my passion earlier in life.

"If you can't figure out your purpose, figure out your passion. For your passion will lead you right into your purpose."

—*Bishop T. D. Jakes*

Resilience

When I visited Myanmar to meet with partners and beneficiaries, I saw powerful examples of resilience every day.

Daw Khin Nwe Oo, a statuesque mom of six, sells sticky rice snacks in her village. As part of our microfinance project, she receives financial and business management training. Quick to smile and laugh, her business does extremely well, enabling her two youngest daughters to remain in school. If she did not have her business, her daughters would have been pulled out of school to work and earn income for the family. Education is vitally important to Daw Khin.

All the women I met in Myanmar touched my heart.

They impressed me with their positive, hopeful attitudes, their resilience in the face of adversity, their confidence, and their self-reliance. They embody my belief that teaching a girl can change the world.

"Resilience is knowing that you are the only one who has the power and the responsibility to pick yourself up."

—Mary Holloway

Creativity

In many cultures, spider webs embody creation and death.
Webs are built by female spiders. She is the creative force,
weaving the designs of life and fate.

Dakota and Lakota native tribes use spider web ornamentation
to represent invincibility and invisibility. Just as an arrow can pass
through a spider web, leaving it intact, so is a warrior wearing the
symbol rendered invincible. And since a spider web is difficult to
see unless it is wet, she is also rendered invisible.

Most spiders use wind power to initiate their web spinning.
They shoot a strand up into the air so the wind can send it aloft
and anchor it. Spiders produce silk strands from tiny organs
on their abdomens. When released, the silk is in liquid form,
but solidifies after contact with air. Web silk is one of the most
high-performance materials known to man. A spider can spin
an elaborate web in an hour, and it will serve as her habitat and
means to catch prey.

"When spider webs unite, they can tie up a lion."

— African proverb

Bumblebee

Bainbridge Island has an abundance of bees and diverse pollination opportunities.

This is a bumblebee. Although she cannot produce honey, her cross-pollination skills are essential to our ecosystem.

With five eyes, she can discern the colors, shapes, and UV markings of flowers as she weaves together her pollen concoctions. Her wingbeat, generating the distinctive vibrating buzz, is the key to her pollination proficiency.

"The bee is more honored than other animals, not because she labors, but because she labors for others."

—Saint John Chrysostom

Aloof

Meet Spike, my neighbors' fearless, aloof, beautiful family member. Spike rules.

Frequently, cats look and act superior, demonstrating that they are in charge and unforgiving of others' mistakes.

Although I am very much a dog person now, I grew up with cats. Smokey was a tabby and had been raised with puppies with whom he learned to enjoy walking in mud puddles. Pokee, a Siamese, appeared one day and stayed for several years. And then he left. When I moved off to college, my brother accidentally backed the car over Smokey. He loved Smokey and felt horrible. He didn't tell me the truth until a few years ago.

"I was drawn to his aloofness, the way cats gravitate toward people who'd rather avoid them."

—Rachel Hartman, Seraphina

Chicks

Bainbridge Island is home to a bounty of chickens and chicken coops. It seems almost every yard has a handful of hens. Even if you do not own chickens, you most likely eat farm fresh eggs.

We have an annual "Tour de Coup" which showcases some of the finest chicken abodes and provides a map to all the coops on the island.

One local entrepreneur, Campbell's Chicken Coop, designs and constructs coops, provides consulting and chicken sitting, and even walks chickens.

The island's local Bay Hay and Feed always sells baby chicks in spring. When I see the adorable soft babies under the warming lights, it is all I can do to resist bringing them home.

"A true friend is someone who thinks you are a good egg."

—Anonymous

Courage

Hearts of Courage posters, a collaborative effort of local elementary school students, pepper Bainbridge Island. They are a constant reminder during Covid-19 of how the pandemic is impacting our children.

Courage is the state of mind and spirit that enables us to face difficulty. We encourage our children to believe that somewhere inside of them, courage is there when they need it, whether they feel it or not. I believe the world's beauty fortifies us with courage to face our fears.

"May the sun bring you new energy by day. May the moon softly restore you by night. May the rain wash away your worries. May the breeze blow new strength into your being. May you walk gently through the world and know its beauty all the days of your life."

—Apache Blessing

HEARTS OF COURAGE

HEARTS CREATED BY WILKES ELEMENTARY STUDENTS

Beachy

Beachy fun

in drizzly rain,

sizzling sun,

or gloomy gray skies.

Cooking up s'mores,

pounding the oars,

fireside chats—

What more?

Fishing for cod,

walking the shore,

riding the waves—

our spirits soar.

Friendship

Friendship has many forms and depths, from acquaintances to life-long bonds. Sometimes, friendships develop through shared interests, such as playing mahjongg. Swapping the tiles, divulging secrets, and laughing together have shaped memories that will forever reside in my heart.

Friendships have been tested during Covid. To protect ourselves and one another from infection, we don masks and have settled for small gatherings, preferably outdoors at a distance. For those living alone, loneliness and depression have taken a toll.

Yet human contact and friendship have never been more essential. Creativity reigns during the pandemic, as we figure out how to nurture existing friendships and reach out to those who need a kind word.

"We are all travelers in the wilderness of this world, and the best we can find in our travels is an honest friend."

—Robert Lewis Stevenson

Smile

I know how happy I feel when someone smiles at me. It can make my day. Data shows that smiles improve our moods and the moods of our smile recipients. Smiles are contagious. Smiles connect us with others.

A "Duchenne smile" is one that includes our eyes, making the corners crinkle up. Even though this is a time when we desperately need to see smiles, we must now wear masks to prevent Covid spread—smiling with our eyes is our only option.

"Your joy can be the source of your smile, but sometimes, your smile can be the source of your joy."

—*Thich Nhat Hanh*

Joy

Colors awaken emotions. These golden dogwood blossoms create a powerful sense of joy within me.

Colors influence my thinking and affect my moods. They can spur action and change reactions. I associate yellow, specifically, with joy, freshness, and intelligence, as it stimulates the logical part of the brain. Though it has a negative side—being known to arouse egotism, deception, and caution—yellow can also inspire creativity, clarity, and curiosity.

"We need joy as we need air. We need love as we need water. We need each other as we need the earth we share."

—Maya Angelou

Raindrops

Raindrops resting on petals

Fallen beads of light

Tumbling from the heavens

Singing songs through the night.

Swollen molecules

Relentless and fierce

Gentle and enchanting

Bouncing on the earth.

Intoxicating freshness

Reviving nature's brilliance

A serendipitous symphony

Of sparkle and delight.

Light

"Follow the Light" is my life mantra. Light draws me in at a glance. To me, light is beauty, hope, warmth, relaxation, and a pathway to a higher power. Sitting outside with the sun warming my face, I talk to my dear friend Linda who passed too early from cancer. It always makes me smile.

Capturing light in my photos is my never-ending quest. I know what I see with my eyes and how it makes me feel, but it is elusive through a lens. When I feel I have been reasonably successful, I am ecstatic.

"For there is always light, if only we are brave enough to see it. If only we are brave enough to be it."

—Amanda Gorman, National Youth Poet Laureate, January 20, 2021, Inauguration Day, "The Hill We Climb"

Vibrance

Awareness of the vibrancy surrounding us through our lives is a powerful concept.

Though the intensity of muted colors, the energy of stillness, and the strength of silence are often difficult to see, they are worth recognizing.

"If we allow ourselves to stay amazed and astounded at the vibrant instants of every day and do not feel ashamed of admitting to being speechless or dumbfounded sometimes, we can uncover unsuspected sparkling gems hidden in the nooks and crannies of our mind."

—Erik Pevernagie, "Skyward, over and above"

Symmetry

Symmetry in architecture and design is relatively easy to spot, as in this photo of the supporting structure under the Bainbridge Island ferry walkway. My eyes are drawn to symmetry because it creates a sense of balance and proportion.

Nature demonstrates symmetry with butterflies. Their wings are identical on the left and right sides. The golden rule, "treat others as you want to be treated," appeals for symmetry in relationships.

When everything matches up, somehow everything feels right with the world. And in the midst of chaos, we search for something still and perfect.

"Symmetry is pleasing but not as sexy. Einstein is cool but Picasso knows what I'm talking about."

—Amy Poehler

Contrasts

Black-and-white photos emphasize contrasts. Punchy is the goal—portraying edginess, high energy, and drama.

Ideally, photos arouse emotions, both for the photographer and the viewer.

When I snapped this photo in color, I saw it in my mind in black and white. And I vividly remember my excitement at finding this scene.

"What good is the warmth of summer, without the cold of winter to give it sweetness? You only truly, deeply appreciate and are grateful for something when you compare and contrast it to something worse."

—John Steinbeck, Travels with Charley: In Search of America

Planet

Remember

Glistening snowcaps

Above lush green forests,

Fields of wheat

Dancing under sparkling blue skies

Our planet's splendor.

Remember

Crystal clear rivers

Nourishing wildlife habitats,

Peaceful weather currents

Ensuring food security chains

Our planet's abundance.

Let us preserve our bounty and

Cultivate our opportunities.

Let us not presume

Nor sit idle

Let us save our planet.

Transitions

I usually associate nature's transitions with spring, when life and light re-emerge.

This former bus stop shelter is transitioning through decomposition. Nature is taking ownership with moss, ferns, decay, and the breakdown of the wooden structure. Decomposition is an essential component of our ecosystem. It is the work of bacteria, fungi, and other microorganisms, and it returns nutrients to the earth to be used again. I have been watching this structure's transition for over twenty years.

"Nature speaks to us through different images, landscapes, colors, patterns, and forms of exquisite beauty. As we admire nature's extravagance, our emotions and feelings become part of it. This harmonious balance makes our souls happy."

—Ralph Waldo Emerson

Earth

There are many parallels between Covid-19 and climate change. Both are global in nature. Neither respect borders. Both are disasters with an environmental origin. Both will cause hundreds of thousands to millions of deaths. Many people still question the legitimacy of both, and no one is immune to the impacts of either. Together, they eat away at us just as rust consumes this old warship buoy.

"To understand the kind of damage that climate change will inflict, look at COVID-19 and spread the pain out over a much longer period."

—Bill Gates

Grounding

Jack Kornfield's guided meditation asks me to visualize roots growing down from my feet, burrowing into the earth like tree roots. The roots stabilize me, even when turbulence invades my mind. This grounding visualization keeps me centered and steady.

"A tree has roots in the soil yet reaches to the sky. It tells us that in order to aspire we need to be grounded and that no matter how high we go it is from our roots that we draw sustenance."

—Wangari Maathai

Wonder

I wander alone and I wonder.

I wonder at this curious creature

What does he think of me

Does he wonder what I might be

What does he see?

I see beauty and curiosity.

Does he see a curious creature

That is me?

I wonder.

Perspective

Perspectives are fluid. Some are more distorted than others.

My perspectives are impacted by current mood, knowledge, personal bias, age, and intentions. My favorite mantra is "keep it in perspective." Basically, what is the relative importance in the grand scheme of life.

"They who dance are thought mad by those who hear not the music."

—Proverb

Magnificence

Having grown up in the Pacific Northwest, Mt. Rainier is an integral background feature in my life. Its striking magnificence never ceases to take away my breath.

    Seen in this augmented photo, I am drawn into its accentuated depths, layering and mysticism, never previously appreciated.

   "I believe the world is incomprehensibly beautiful — an endless prospect of magic and wonder."

   –Ansel Adams

Reflection

In photography, reflection is powerful. It captures an image within an image. At first glance, this view from Bloedel Reserve looks like it is upside down because the sky is on the bottom. However, it is just an illusion.

Mirrors give me feedback on who I am and what I am experiencing in the moment. The reflection reaffirms my sense of self.

Some people purposefully smile at themselves in the mirror each morning to lift their spirits. An illusion made real.

I sometimes rely on other people as my mirrors. They reflect the parts of me I am unable to see, and this awareness is powerful.

"You're always with yourself, so you might as well enjoy the company."

—Diane von Furstenberg

Balance

Walking across this log would require an equal distribution of weight, a physical and mental balance.

Photographic balance, when symmetry, color, tone, and conceptual techniques move a viewer's eye around an image without resting too heavily on any one element, creates a sense of satisfaction.

Nature's balance, when the relationships of organisms to each other and their environment are harmonious and integrated, results in a healthy ecosystem.

Buddhists believe in the Middle Way, a form of balance, referring to an equal amount of effort and concentration. A balanced life creates contentment, peace, and happiness.

"A well-developed sense of humor is the pole that adds balance to your steps as you walk the tightrope of life."

—*William Arthur Ward*

Awakening

"The Lame Goat" by Rumi

You've seen a herd of goats

going down to the water.

The lame and dreamy goat

brings up the rear.

There are worried faces about that one,

but now they're laughing,

because look, as they return,

that goat is leading!

There are many different kinds of knowing.

The lame goat's kind is a branch

that traces back to the roots of presence.

Learn from the lame goat,

and lead the herd home.

Remains

Bygone days

huddled by the fire

rustling up supper

disclosing dreams and desires—

memories abound.

Today's remains—

rising waters

snaking ivy

nooks and crannies.

Still standing.

Still strong.

Mount Rainier

A masterpiece takes time, especially a masterpiece of nature.

At 14,411 feet, Mount Rainier serves as a visual beacon within the Pacific Northwest. Originally named Tahoma by local tribes, it is the "mountain that was god." This volcanic mountain has not erupted since 1894, but is still considered active and potentially deadly. The starkness of its glaciers is offset magically by fields of vibrant wildflowers softly dancing in the wind.

"We call upon the mountains, the Cascades and the Olympics, the high green valleys and meadows filled with wild flowers, the snows that never melt, the summits of intense silence, and we ask that they teach us, and show us the way."

—Chinook blessing

Flapper

First, I hear the loud, deep, musical ah-honk echoing around me. Looking to the sky, I spy a glorious expansive V of Canadian geese. These elegant waterfowl use their voices generously when excited or inadvertently separated from their flock. Flapping, when not taking flight, is a sign of delight. They molt annually in summer and lose all their flying feathers simultaneously—unable to fly for several weeks. Finally, families become able to migrate in flocks to the Pacific coastal regions. The magic of their knowledge is that flight routes and seasonal home locations are passed along by parents to babies during a single migration!

"One swallow does not make a summer, but one skein of geese, cleaving the murk of March thaw, is the Spring."

—Aldo Leopold

Path

I have learned through my seventy-four years of life that there are countless paths we shall walk. We can never truly anticipate the twists and turns. For me, the biggest surprise was learning at age sixty-five that I had been adopted at birth. Yes, my wonderful, loving adopted family could really keep a secret!

As overwhelming and anxiety-ridden as this discovery was, the exceptional outcome was a loving sister—a true blessing.

"I will not follow where the path may lead, but I will go where there is no path, and I will leave a trail."

—Muriel Strode

Labyrinth

An ancient symbol, labyrinths have long been used as meditation and prayer tools. Bainbridge Island's Halls Hill Labyrinth sits at a peaceful vista overlooking Blakely Harbor. A single continuous walkway, the labyrinth combines circles and spirals into a meandering yet purposeful path. Walking the labyrinth can release old patterned behavior, creating a shift in our spiritual alignments.

"It is best to walk the labyrinth with an open heart and an open mind, asking for that which is for your highest good."

—Anonymous

Tapestry

I love the visual of sweet and bittersweet choices and actions woven together, forming a patchwork quilt that is my life. Choices that were heartrending or felt wrong brought revelations that created hope and resilience. Choices that brought unexpected joy and love were a true gift. All have been essential in creating this beautiful paradox that is life.

"As I look back at the entire tapestry of my life, I can see from the perspective of the present moment that every aspect of my life was necessary and perfect. Each step eventually led to a higher place, even though these steps often felt like obstacles or painful experiences."

—*Wayne Dyer, Real Magic*

Hope

Believing there is light at the end of the tunnel inspires hope. Now that Covid vaccines are available, I can see the light. It is still far away, but shining brighter every day.

The power of hope keeps me going when times are tough, helps me persevere, and gives me strength and courage. It reminds me that this, too, shall pass.

Psychologists say that hope is an emotion that springs from the heart, not the brain. It lays dormant until its strength is beckoned. Emily Dickinson says:

Hope is the thing with feathers –

that perches in the soul –

and sings the tune without the words –

and never stops – at all –

CPSIA information can be obtained
at www.ICGtesting.com
Printed in the USA
LVHW070404040521
686390LV00002B/2

* 9 7 8 0 5 7 8 9 0 0 8 3 4 *